The People Of Proverbs Application For Life Series . . .

The Fine Art Of Experiencing Quality Relationships

31 Intentional Days Of Thoughtful Treasures From Proverbs
That Will Transform The Heart

Daily Declarations For Positive People

Based On, Today May You In Proverbs:
The Quality Leader's Essential Guidebook For
Personal, Professional, and Spiritual Growth

By Dr. Denny Bates

The Fine Art Of Experiencing Quality Relationships:
31 Intentional Days Of Thoughtful Treasures From Proverbs
That Will Transform The Heart

Today May You In Proverbs

The Quality Leader's Essential Guidebook For

Personal, Professional, and Spiritual Growth

Something New Christian Publishers
E-Mail dennybates@gmail.com
On the Web: www.dennybates.com

You can "friend" me on Facebook at www.facebook.com/denny.bates
or follow me on Twitter @dennybates
www.TheQualityDisciple.com

Table Of Contents

The Fine Art Of Experiencing Quality Relationships

Preface

WHY is "The Fine Art Of Experiencing Quality Relationships" just the book for you?

I believe this book will change minds and hearts. *The Fine Art Of Experiencing Quality Relationship*: addresses every significant subject that matters in this Modern Age. From Abundance to Poverty, from taking Advice to the Pride that rejects it, from being Blessed to suffering a Curse, from Dreams to Destiny, from Encouragement to Depression, from Friends to Enemies, from Love to Hatred, from a Happy Heart to a Broken Heart, from Humility to Haughtiness, from Integrity to Dishonesty, from Justice realized to Justice unfulfilled, from intentional Leadership to a disastrous lack of Character, from telling the Truth to telling a Lie, from Life to Death, from guided Mentorship to a life that has no Direction at all, and from a healthy Biblical view of Sex and Love to a perverted version of Sex and Love. It's all there in Proverbs.

And above all of those examples, how to best experience QUALITY RELATIONSHIPS is distinctly spelled out. Everything that really matters, a precise Biblical blueprint for a successful life, is made clear within the confines of Proverbs to the Quality Leader and to the Quality Disciple.

Even in modern times like these, the ancient Proverbs remain current for life's greatest issues, including The Fine Art Of Experiencing Quality Relationships. They are **Practical**. They are easily understood and then applied.

They are **Panoramic**. As mentioned above, the breadth and depth of life topics run the gamut.

They are **Perceptive**. The Spirit is your guide as He gives you sensitive insight into the nuggets of wisdom that will transform your life.

Practical / Panoramic / Perceptive = PROVERBS

Dedication

Every now and then, there are people who have come into my life that have brought immense value to me, both personally, professionally, and even spiritually. Rare is the case where the same person contributes to all three in such a profound kind of way.

I met David Fountain and his wife Sheila years ago at the church we attended. It did not take long for David and me to realize that a special bond of friendship was taking place between us. At his core, he is an entrepreneur who quickly realized the impact in the marketplace he could make as a businessman who was also a committed Christian. In David's heart, he has a passion for excellence in leadership: excellence in his personal life, his professional life, and in his spiritual life too.

I am honored to have become a "spiritual father" to David as well his business coach too. For years he was in a group we affectionately called DM4J (DiscipleMakers4Jesus) where several other men challenged each other to grow in their faith and love for Jesus. It is true that iron does sharpen iron.

The more I worked with David, the more I grew too! I grew as a business coach. When I began to expand my horizons beyond the church world, David was one of the first business clients that trusted me with both himself AND his business. Looking back, it was a blessing to see David's growth as a leader of several UPS Store franchises in South Carolina.

But most of all, I'm grateful for the spiritual friendship we have forged over the years. When many friends over the years have come and gone, David has displayed such loyalty to me. And so, it's my pleasure to dedicate this book about quality relationships to David Fountain.

Dr. Denny Bates
September 2020

Acknowledgements

My books are so much better because of those who willingly volunteer their time to read through the sample proof and make sure, first and foremost, that the contents speak to the heart first and then to the mind. They are also people of good grammar and watch out for those pesky typos that get by me, but not them. I am grateful to Leigh Ann Wheeler, Bryan Braddock, Amy Watts, Reeves Cannon, Dick Brown, Tamara Rhodes, Lisa Ray, Traci McCombs, Amy Clark, Ron Lyles, Wick Jackson, Patty Smith, Leslie Rutten, Laura Harris, Cleo Corey, Carol Mabe, and Kirby King.

'Every time I think of you, I give thanks to my God. Whenever I pray, I make my requests for all of you with joy, for you have been my partners in spreading the Good News about Christ from the time you first heard it until now. And I am certain that God, who began the good work within you, will continue his work until it is finally finished on the day when Christ Jesus returns.'

Philippians 1:3-6

FOREWORD

I met Dr. Denny Bates in February 2020, only 18 months after watching my husband of 37 years take a tragic and fatal fall. Over the course of my friendship with Denny, he has walked me through areas of grief, identity, and most importantly, spiritual discipleship. He has taught and modeled how to pray through and study the Scriptures.

We began studying Proverbs through his book *31 Intentional Days Of Life Transformation.* As we studied Proverbs together, the Scriptures came alive. The workbook-style of the book allowed me to dig deeper, as I was able to mark key words, research other Scriptures, and make applications to my life. I soon found myself having a hunger for God's Word like I had not experienced in many years.

If you could benefit from a life coach, or just want to learn how to better approach life through the Scriptures, I highly recommend my friend and mentor, Dr. Denny Bates

Leigh Ann Wheeler

What Notable Theologians Say About the Book of Proverbs

Charles Spurgeon on The Book of Proverbs:

"The Proverbs appear at first sight to be thrown together without connection, but it is not so: when you come to close reading you will discover that they are threaded pearls, and that they are in proper position with regard to each other."

Billy Graham on the Book of Proverbs:

"The Psalms tell us how to get along with God, and the Proverbs tell us how to get along with our fellow man."

Nate Pickowicz on the Book of Proverbs:

"The beautiful thing about the wisdom of Proverbs is that it's timeless. While textbooks often need updating, Proverbs hasn't had a 2nd edition in three millennia!"

The Book of Proverbs *is* the pathway towards Growing in Greatness!

[5] Trust in the LORD with all your heart; do not depend on your own understanding.
[6] Seek his will in all you do, and he will show you which path to take.
Proverbs 3:5-6 (NLT)

"God does not give us everything we want, but He does fulfill His promises, leading us along the best and straightest paths to Himself." – **Dietrich Bonhoeffer**

This wonderful and timeless book of Proverbs will be the path that will, as Bonhoeffer says, lead us along the best and straightest paths to Himself.

QUALITY QUOTES FOR THE QUALITY LEADER
WHO DESIRES TO GROW:

"Transformation is not five minutes from now; it's a present activity. In this moment you can make a different choice, and it's these small choices and successes that build up over time to help cultivate a healthy self-image and self-esteem." —JILLIAN MICHAELS

"Transformation literally means going beyond your form." —WAYNE DYER

"Transformation is a process, and as life happens there are tons of ups and downs.
It's a journey of discovery." —RICK WARREN

"Income seldom exceeds personal development." —JIM ROHN

"You cannot dream yourself into a character; you must hammer and forge yourself one."
—HENRY DAVID THOREAU

"Personal development is a major time-saver. The better you become, the less time it takes you to achieve your goals." —BRIAN TRACY

"The only person you are destined to become is the person you decide to be."
—RALPH WALDO EMERSON

"There is nothing noble in being superior to your fellow man; true nobility is being superior to your former self." —ERNEST HEMINGWAY

"When we are no longer able to change a situation, we are challenged to change ourselves."
—VIKTOR E. FRANKL

"Of course motivation is not permanent. But then, neither is bathing; but it is something you should do on a regular basis." – ZIG ZIGLAR

"As the physically weak man can make himself strong by careful and patient training, so the man of weak thoughts can make them strong by exercising himself in right thinking." – *JAMES ALLEN*

"Growth is the great separator between those who succeed and those who do not. When I see a person beginning to separate themselves from the pack, it's almost always due to personal growth."
—JOHN C. MAXWELL

'And I am certain that God, who began the good work within you, will continue his work until it is finally finished on the day when Christ Jesus returns.' (Philippians 1:6 NLT) –*THE APOSTLE PAUL*

'But if you remain in me and my words remain in you, you may ask for anything you want, and it will be granted! When you produce much fruit, you are my true disciples. This brings great glory to my Father.' (John 15:7-8 NLT)—*JESUS*

Some Suggestions On How To Use The Fine Art Of Experiencing Quality Relationships:

- You can use this spiritual growth resource as a daily devotion. It is designed as a tool you can use as a devotion and a Bible study: You can use it in the morning before you begin your day and at night, at the end of your day. *You can also customize this resource and turn it into a small group study!*

- Contained in each devotional entry is The Day, The Title of The Devotion, The Proverb, The Positive Confession of "Today May You," and then the Declaration Of Quality Wisdom written as a Prayer Of Commitment.

- This spiritual growth resource is set up as a thirty-one-day exercise, it can be adapted to your lifestyle. In other words, use what you need and then set aside the rest for another time. Your goal is not speed. Your goal needs to be spiritual growth.

If you decide you want to take the daily approach, here is what you will experience:

- A passage of Scripture you can read and then let it set your spiritual framework for the rest of the day. Look for <u>key words</u> and <u>phrases</u> that you can mull over.

- For each daily Scripture there also is a *"Declaration Of Quality Wisdom"* which is your declaration for the day. It may help you better grasp the power of what you are reading by reading it aloud several times at the beginning and throughout the day.

- After you read the declaration you will be invited to personalize your declaration by offering it as a prayer. It might help you to also read this prayer aloud. Resist the temptation to rush through this spiritual experience. Words have meaning. Ponder each one of these precious words as you pray over each one.

- On the page are Bible study prompts that will guide you to a deeper learning experience by going through the process of OBSERVATION, INTERPRETATION, and APPLICATION of the Bible passage.

Okay! Let's begin your journey into living out the great promises of *The Fine Art Of Experiencing Quality Relationships*. Your next step towards spiritual growth begins on the next page.

DAY ONE: "Winning Friendships"

Today May You . . . make it your goal to ADD VALUE to everyone you meet.

The seeds of good deeds become a tree of life;

a wise person wins friends. (Proverbs 11:30 NLT).

Turn your *Declaration Of Quality Wisdom* into this prayer of commitment:

> Lord Jesus, ***Today May I*** make it my goal to ADD VALUE to everyone I meet.

 **Going Deeper**

Observation: What is the writer of Proverbs saying *{Look for key words, doctrines, unique phrases}?*

Interpretation: What does it mean? *{If you are doing a word study you may want to use a concordance. If you are studying a doctrine (a Biblical principle), can you give it a name? i.e., "the doctrine of . . . "}*

Application: What is God is saying to my heart? What is my next step in applying this truth? *{This is a key part of your Bible study. Read and pray through the Proverb again and review your thoughts on your notes on Observation and Interpretation then write out a concise personal application.}*

Proclamation: Take a moment. Ponder this and pray. Then answer this question: Who needs to hear this insight from me?

Personal Journal Notes And Prayer Concerns

DAY TWO: "Live The Life You Believe"

Today May You . . . THINK good thoughts, do good DEEDS, and make a good CONTRIBUTION to your community.

The Lord approves of those who are good,

but he condemns those who plan wickedness.

Wickedness never brings stability,

but the godly have deep roots. (Proverbs 12:2-3 NLT).

Turn your *Declaration Of Quality Wisdom* into this prayer of commitment:

> Lord Jesus, ***Today May I*** THINK good thoughts, do good DEEDS, and make a good CONTRIBUTION to my community.

 **Going Deeper**

Observation: What is the writer of Proverbs saying *{Look for key words, doctrines, unique phrases}?*

Interpretation: What does it mean? *{If you are doing a word study you may want to use a concordance. If you are studying a doctrine (a Biblical principle), can you give it a name? i.e., "the doctrine of . . . "}*

Application: What is God is saying to my heart? What is my next step in applying this truth? *{This is a key part of your Bible study. Read and pray through the Proverb again and review your thoughts on your notes on Observation and Interpretation then write out a concise personal application.}*

Proclamation: Take a moment. Ponder this and pray. Then answer this question: Who needs to hear this insight from me?

Personal Journal Notes And Prayer Concerns

DAY THREE: "Harnessing The Power Of Your Plans And Your Words"

Today May You . . . add value to others by how you PLAN and by what you SAY.

The plans of the godly are just;

the advice of the wicked is treacherous.

The words of the wicked are like a murderous ambush,

but the words of the godly save lives. (Proverbs 12:5-6 NLT).

Turn your *Declaration Of Quality Wisdom* **into this prayer of commitment:**

Lord Jesus, *Today May I* add value to others by how I PLAN and by what I SAY.

 **Going Deeper**

Observation: What is the writer of Proverbs saying *{Look for key words, doctrines, unique phrases}?*

Interpretation: What does it mean? *{If you are doing a word study you may want to use a concordance. If you are studying a doctrine (a Biblical principle), can you give it a name? i.e., "the doctrine of . . . "}*

Application: What is God is saying to my heart? What is my next step in applying this truth? *{This is a key part of your Bible study. Read and pray through the Proverb again and review your thoughts on your notes on Observation and Interpretation then write out a concise personal application.}*

Proclamation: Take a moment. Ponder this and pray. Then answer this question: Who needs to hear this insight from me?

Personal Journal Notes And Prayer Concerns

DAY FOUR: "The Results Of Choosing To Live An Intentional Life"

Today May You . . . be INTENTIONAL on using wise words and working hard so you may be SUCCESSFUL.

Wise words bring many benefits,
and hard work brings rewards. (Proverbs 12:14 NLT).

Turn your *Declaration Of Quality Wisdom* into this prayer of commitment:

Lord Jesus, ***Today May I*** be INTENTIONAL on using wise words and working hard so I may be SUCCESSFUL.

 **Going Deeper**

Observation: What is the writer of Proverbs saying *{Look for key words, doctrines, unique phrases}?*

Interpretation: What does it mean? *{If you are doing a word study you may want to use a concordance. If you are studying a doctrine (a Biblical principle), can you give it a name? i.e., "the doctrine of . . . "}*

Application: What is God is saying to my heart? What is my next step in applying this truth? *{This is a key part of your Bible study. Read and pray through the Proverb again and review your thoughts on your notes on Observation and Interpretation then write out a concise personal application.}*

Proclamation: Take a moment. Ponder this and pray. Then answer this question: Who needs to hear this insight from me?

Personal Journal Notes And Prayer Concerns

DAY FIVE: "The Blessing Of Passing On Good Advice"

Today May You . . . be willing to SPEAK the truth and ENCOURAGE your friends to make the kinds of choices that will add great VALUE to them.

The godly give good advice to their friends; the wicked lead them astray. (Proverbs 12:26 NLT).

Turn your *Declaration Of Quality Wisdom* into this prayer of commitment:

Lord Jesus, ***Today May I*** be willing to SPEAK the truth and ENCOURAGE my friends to make the kinds of choices that will add great VALUE to them.

 **Going Deeper**

Observation: What is the writer of Proverbs saying *{Look for key words, doctrines, unique phrases}?*

Interpretation: What does it mean? *{If you are doing a word study you may want to use a concordance. If you are studying a doctrine (a Biblical principle), can you give it a name? i.e., "the doctrine of . . . "}*

Application: What is God is saying to my heart? What is my next step in applying this truth? *{This is a key part of your Bible study. Read and pray through the Proverb again and review your thoughts on your notes on Observation and Interpretation then write out a concise personal application.}*

Proclamation: Take a moment. Ponder this and pray. Then answer this question: Who needs to hear this insight from me?

Personal Journal Notes And Prayer Concerns

DAY SIX: "The Blessing Of Having A Humble Heart"

Today May You . . . have a HEART of HUMILITY that will be open to ADVICE so you can SUCCEED.

People who despise advice are asking for trouble;

those who respect a command will succeed. (Proverbs 13:13 NLT).

Turn your *Declaration Of Quality Wisdom* into this prayer of commitment:

Lord Jesus, ***Today May I*** have a HEART of HUMILITY that will be open to ADVICE So that I can SUCCEED.

 **Going Deeper**

Observation: What is the writer of Proverbs saying *{Look for key words, doctrines, unique phrases}?*

Interpretation: What does it mean? *{If you are doing a word study you may want to use a concordance. If you are studying a doctrine (a Biblical principle), can you give it a name? i.e., "the doctrine of . . . "}*

Application: What is God is saying to my heart? What is my next step in applying this truth? *{This is a key part of your Bible study. Read and pray through the Proverb again and review your thoughts on your notes on Observation and Interpretation then write out a concise personal application.}*

Proclamation: Take a moment. Ponder this and pray. Then answer this question: Who needs to hear this insight from me?

Personal Journal Notes And Prayer Concerns

DAY SEVEN: "Why Wisdom Works"

Today May You . . . be WISE enough to listen to the advice of WISE people and make WISE decisions that will be a blessing to you.

The instruction of the wise is like a life-giving fountain;

those who accept it avoid the snares of death. (Proverbs 13:14 NLT).

Turn your *Declaration Of Quality Wisdom* into this prayer of commitment:

Lord Jesus, **_Today May I_** be WISE enough to listen to the advice of WISE people and make WISE decisions that will be a blessing to me.

Going Deeper

Observation: What is the writer of Proverbs saying *{Look for key words, doctrines, unique phrases}?*

Interpretation: What does it mean? *{If you are doing a word study you may want to use a concordance. If you are studying a doctrine (a Biblical principle), can you give it a name? i.e., "the doctrine of . . . "}*

Application: What is God is saying to my heart? What is my next step in applying this truth? *{This is a key part of your Bible study. Read and pray through the Proverb again and review your thoughts on your notes on Observation and Interpretation then write out a concise personal application.}*

Proclamation: Take a moment. Ponder this and pray. Then answer this question: Who needs to hear this insight from me?

Personal Journal Notes And Prayer Concerns

DAY EIGHT: "Before You Leap"

Today May You . . . before you do anything, THINK, PRAY, LISTEN, and then ACT.

Wise people think before they act;

fools don't—and even brag about their foolishness. (Proverbs 13:16 NLT).

Turn your *Declaration Of Quality Wisdom* into this prayer of commitment:

Lord Jesus, ***Today May I*** before I do anything, THINK, PRAY, LISTEN, and then ACT.

 **Going Deeper**

Observation: What is the writer of Proverbs saying *{Look for key words, doctrines, unique phrases}?*

Interpretation: What does it mean? *{If you are doing a word study you may want to use a concordance. If you are studying a doctrine (a Biblical principle), can you give it a name? i.e., "the doctrine of . . ."}*

Application: What is God is saying to my heart? What is my next step in applying this truth? *{This is a key part of your Bible study. Read and pray through the Proverb again and review your thoughts on your notes on Observation and Interpretation then write out a concise personal application.}*

Proclamation: Take a moment. Ponder this and pray. Then answer this question: Who needs to hear this insight from me?

Personal Journal Notes And Prayer Concerns

DAY NINE: "Why Being Open To Correction Will Open Doors For You"

Today May You . . . have an open MIND to learn more, an open HEART to change more and an open LIFE to show more of God's grace at work in you.

If you ignore criticism, you will end in poverty and disgrace;

if you accept correction, you will be honored. (Proverbs 13:18 NLT).

Turn your *Declaration Of Quality Wisdom* **into this prayer of commitment:**

> Lord Jesus, *Today May I* have an open MIND to learn more, an open HEART to change more and an open LIFE to show more of God's grace at work in me.

 **Going Deeper**

Observation: What is the writer of Proverbs saying *{Look for key words, doctrines, unique phrases}?*

Interpretation: What does it mean? *{If you are doing a word study you may want to use a concordance. If you are studying a doctrine (a Biblical principle), can you give it a name? i.e., "the doctrine of . . . "}*

Application: What is God is saying to my heart? What is my next step in applying this truth? *{This is a key part of your Bible study. Read and pray through the Proverb again and review your thoughts on your notes on Observation and Interpretation then write out a concise personal application.}*

Proclamation: Take a moment. Ponder this and pray. Then answer this question: Who needs to hear this insight from me?

Personal Journal Notes And Prayer Concerns

DAY TEN: "Under Advisement"

Today May You . . . always get better advice than your own.

Plans go wrong for lack of advice;

many advisers bring success. (Proverbs 15:22 NLT).

Turn your *Declaration Of Quality Wisdom* into this prayer of commitment:

Lord Jesus, **Today May I** always get better advice than my own.

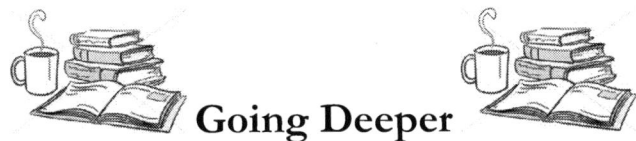 **Going Deeper**

Observation: What is the writer of Proverbs saying *{Look for key words, doctrines, unique phrases}?*

Interpretation: What does it mean? *{If you are doing a word study you may want to use a concordance. If you are studying a doctrine (a Biblical principle), can you give it a name? i.e., "the doctrine of . . . "}*

Application: What is God is saying to my heart? What is my next step in applying this truth? *{This is a key part of your Bible study. Read and pray through the Proverb again and review your thoughts on your notes on Observation and Interpretation then write out a concise personal application.}*

Proclamation: Take a moment. Ponder this and pray. Then answer this question: Who needs to hear this insight from me?

Personal Journal Notes And Prayer Concerns

DAY ELEVEN: "Right Of Way"

Today May You . . . say the RIGHT THING at the RIGHT TIME in the RIGHT WAY to the RIGHT PERSON.

Everyone enjoys a fitting reply;

it is wonderful to say the right thing at the right time! (Proverbs 15:23 NLT).

Turn your _Declaration Of Quality Wisdom_ into this prayer of commitment:

Lord Jesus, **_Today May I_** say the RIGHT THING at the RIGHT TIME in the RIGHT WAY to the RIGHT PERSON.

 **Going Deeper**

Observation: What is the writer of Proverbs saying _{Look for key words, doctrines, unique phrases}?_

Interpretation: What does it mean? _{If you are doing a word study you may want to use a concordance. If you are studying a doctrine (a Biblical principle), can you give it a name? i.e., "the doctrine of . . . "}_

Application: What is God is saying to my heart? What is my next step in applying this truth? *{This is a key part of your Bible study. Read and pray through the Proverb again and review your thoughts on your notes on Observation and Interpretation then write out a concise personal application.}*

Proclamation: Take a moment. Ponder this and pray. Then answer this question: Who needs to hear this insight from me?

Personal Journal Notes And Prayer Concerns

DAY TWELVE: "No Gossip Zone"

Today May You . . . make sure every word you use builds someone up and does not take them down.

A troublemaker plants seeds of strife;

gossip separates the best of friends. (Proverbs 16:28 NLT).

Turn your *Declaration Of Quality Wisdom* into this prayer of commitment:

> Lord Jesus, ***Today May I*** make sure every word I use builds someone up and does not take them down.

 **Going Deeper**

Observation: What is the writer of Proverbs saying *{Look for key words, doctrines, unique phrases}?*

Interpretation: What does it mean? *{If you are doing a word study you may want to use a concordance. If you are studying a doctrine (a Biblical principle), can you give it a name? i.e., "the doctrine of . . . "}*

Application: What is God is saying to my heart? What is my next step in applying this truth? *{This is a key part of your Bible study. Read and pray through the Proverb again and review your thoughts on your notes on Observation and Interpretation then write out a concise personal application.}*

Proclamation: Take a moment. Ponder this and pray. Then answer this question: Who needs to hear this insight from me?

Personal Journal Notes And Prayer Concerns

DAY THIRTEEN: "When Tolerance Is Spelled L-O-V-E"

Today May You . . . FORGIVE when you find a FAULT, LOVE when you would rather LASH out, and GIVE GRACE because you need it too.

Love prospers when a fault is forgiven,

but dwelling on it separates close friends. (Proverbs 17:9 NLT).

Turn your *Declaration Of Quality Wisdom* into this prayer of commitment:

> Lord Jesus, ***Today May I*** FORGIVE when I find a FAULT, LOVE when I would rather LASH out, and GIVE GRACE because I need it too.

 **Going Deeper**

Observation: What is the writer of Proverbs saying *{Look for key words, doctrines, unique phrases}?*

Interpretation: What does it mean? *{If you are doing a word study you may want to use a concordance. If you are studying a doctrine (a Biblical principle), can you give it a name? i.e., "the doctrine of . . . "}*

Application: What is God is saying to my heart? What is my next step in applying this truth? *{This is a key part of your Bible study. Read and pray through the Proverb again and review your thoughts on your notes on Observation and Interpretation then write out a concise personal application.}*

Proclamation: Take a moment. Ponder this and pray. Then answer this question: Who needs to hear this insight from me?

Personal Journal Notes And Prayer Concerns

DAY FOURTEEN: "Connect With Me And Then Correct Me"

Today May You . . . be willing to receive CORRECTION when a CORRECTION is needed.

A single rebuke does more for a person of understanding

than a hundred lashes on the back of a fool. (Proverbs 17:10 NLT).

Turn your *Declaration Of Quality Wisdom* into this prayer of commitment:

> Lord Jesus, ***Today May I*** be willing to receive CORRECTION when a
> CORRECTION is needed.

 **Going Deeper**

Observation: What is the writer of Proverbs saying *{Look for key words, doctrines, unique phrases}?*

Interpretation: What does it mean? *{If you are doing a word study you may want to use a concordance. If you are studying a doctrine (a Biblical principle), can you give it a name? i.e., "the doctrine of . . . "}*

Application: What is God is saying to my heart? What is my next step in applying this truth? *{This is a key part of your Bible study. Read and pray through the Proverb again and review your thoughts on your notes on Observation and Interpretation then write out a concise personal application.}*

Proclamation: Take a moment. Ponder this and pray. Then answer this question: Who needs to hear this insight from me?

Personal Journal Notes And Prayer Concerns

DAY FIFTEEN: "The Best Way To Stop An Argument Is Not To Start One"

Today May You . . . control your tongue so your life may be flooded with peace.

Starting a quarrel is like opening a floodgate,

so stop before a dispute breaks out. (Proverbs 17:14 NLT).

Turn your *Declaration Of Quality Wisdom* **into this prayer of commitment:**

Lord Jesus, ***Today May I*** control my tongue so my life may be flooded with peace.

 **Going Deeper**

Observation: What is the writer of Proverbs saying *{Look for key words, doctrines, unique phrases}?*

Interpretation: What does it mean? *{If you are doing a word study you may want to use a concordance. If you are studying a doctrine (a Biblical principle), can you give it a name? i.e., "the doctrine of . . . "}*

Application: What is God is saying to my heart? What is my next step in applying this truth? *{This is a key part of your Bible study. Read and pray through the Proverb again and review your thoughts on your notes on Observation and Interpretation then write out a concise personal application.}*

Proclamation: Take a moment. Ponder this and pray. Then answer this question: Who needs to hear this insight from me?

Personal Journal Notes And Prayer Concerns

DAY SIXTEEN: "The Best Kind Of Friend"

Today May You . . . be the kind of friend you need to be for you.

A friend is always loyal,

and a brother is born to help in time of need. (Proverbs 17:17 NLT).

Turn your *Declaration Of Quality Wisdom* into this prayer of commitment:

Lord Jesus, ***Today May I*** be the kind of friend I need to be for me.

 **Going Deeper**

Observation: What is the writer of Proverbs saying *{Look for key words, doctrines, unique phrases}?*

Interpretation: What does it mean? *{If you are doing a word study you may want to use a concordance. If you are studying a doctrine (a Biblical principle), can you give it a name? i.e., "the doctrine of . . . "}*

Application: What is God is saying to my heart? What is my next step in applying this truth? *{This is a key part of your Bible study. Read and pray through the Proverb again and review your thoughts on your notes on Observation and Interpretation then write out a concise personal application.}*

Proclamation: Take a moment. Ponder this and pray. Then answer this question: Who needs to hear this insight from me?

Personal Journal Notes And Prayer Concerns

DAY SEVENTEEN: "Crazy Money"

Today May You . . . not allow your HEART to get ahead of your HEAD or you might lose more than your MIND.

It's poor judgment to guarantee another person's debt
or put up security for a friend. (Proverbs 17:18 NLT).

Turn your *Declaration Of Quality Wisdom* **into this prayer of commitment:**

Lord Jesus, *Today May I* not allow my HEART to get ahead of my HEAD or I might lose more than my MIND.

 **Going Deeper**

Observation: What is the writer of Proverbs saying *{Look for key words, doctrines, unique phrases}?*

Interpretation: What does it mean? *{If you are doing a word study you may want to use a concordance. If you are studying a doctrine (a Biblical principle), can you give it a name? i.e., "the doctrine of . . . "}*

Application: What is God is saying to my heart? What is my next step in applying this truth? *{This is a key part of your Bible study. Read and pray through the Proverb again and review your thoughts on your notes on Observation and Interpretation then write out a concise personal application.}*

Proclamation: Take a moment. Ponder this and pray. Then answer this question: Who needs to hear this insight from me?

Personal Journal Notes And Prayer Concerns

DAY EIGHTEEN: "The Winner Takes It All"

Today May You . . . protect the relationships that are important to you by winning their love, not by winning the argument.

An offended friend is harder to win back than a fortified city.
Arguments separate friends like a gate locked with bars. (Proverbs 18:19 NLT).

Turn your *Declaration Of Quality Wisdom* into this prayer of commitment:

> Lord Jesus, ***Today May I*** protect the relationships that are important to me by winning their love, not by winning the argument.

 **Going Deeper**

Observation: What is the writer of Proverbs saying *{Look for key words, doctrines, unique phrases}?*

Interpretation: What does it mean? *{If you are doing a word study you may want to use a concordance. If you are studying a doctrine (a Biblical principle), can you give it a name? i.e., "the doctrine of . . . "}*

Application: What is God is saying to my heart? What is my next step in applying this truth? *{This is a key part of your Bible study. Read and pray through the Proverb again and review your thoughts on your notes on Observation and Interpretation then write out a concise personal application.}*

Proclamation: Take a moment. Ponder this and pray. Then answer this question: Who needs to hear this insight from me?

Personal Journal Notes And Prayer Concerns

DAY NINETEEN: "What Real Friends Do"

Today May You . . . be the kind of trusted friend your intimate circle of friends needs from you.

There are "friends" who destroy each other,

but a real friend sticks closer than a brother. (Proverbs 18:24 NLT).

Turn your *Declaration Of Quality Wisdom* into this prayer of commitment:

Lord Jesus, ***Today May I*** be the kind of trusted friend my intimate circle of friends needs from me.

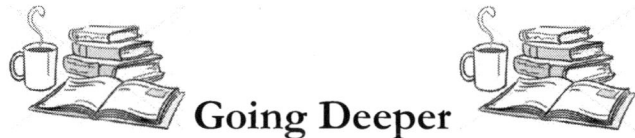 **Going Deeper**

Observation: What is the writer of Proverbs saying *{Look for key words, doctrines, unique phrases}?*

Interpretation: What does it mean? *{If you are doing a word study you may want to use a concordance. If you are studying a doctrine (a Biblical principle), can you give it a name? i.e., "the doctrine of . . . "}*

Application: What is God is saying to my heart? What is my next step in applying this truth? *{This is a key part of your Bible study. Read and pray through the Proverb again and review your thoughts on your notes on Observation and Interpretation then write out a concise personal application.}*

Proclamation: Take a moment. Ponder this and pray. Then answer this question: Who needs to hear this insight from me?

Personal Journal Notes And Prayer Concerns

DAY TWENTY: "Good To Have A Good Friend For Good"

Today May You . . . be a GOOD FRIEND by being a GOOD LISTENER so you will be able to give GOOD ADVICE that will help your friend have a GOOD DAY.

Though good advice lies deep within the heart,
a person with understanding will draw it out. (Proverbs 20:5 NLT).

Turn your *Declaration Of Quality Wisdom* into this prayer of commitment:

Lord Jesus, ***Today May I*** be a GOOD FRIEND by being a GOOD LISTENER so I will be able to give GOOD ADVICE that will help my friend have a GOOD DAY.

 **Going Deeper**

Observation: What is the writer of Proverbs saying *{Look for key words, doctrines, unique phrases}?*

Interpretation: What does it mean? *{If you are doing a word study you may want to use a concordance. If you are studying a doctrine (a Biblical principle), can you give it a name? i.e., "the doctrine of . . . "}*

Application: What is God is saying to my heart? What is my next step in applying this truth? *{This is a key part of your Bible study. Read and pray through the Proverb again and review your thoughts on your notes on Observation and Interpretation then write out a concise personal application.}*

Proclamation: Take a moment. Ponder this and pray. Then answer this question: Who needs to hear this insight from me?

Personal Journal Notes And Prayer Concerns

DAY TWENTY-ONE: "Friendship Qualities That Matter"

Today May You . . . be the most LOYAL and RELIABLE friend you know.

Many will say they are loyal friends,

but who can find one who is truly reliable? (Proverbs 20:6 NLT).

Turn your *Declaration Of Quality Wisdom* into this prayer of commitment:

Lord Jesus, ***Today May I*** be the most LOYAL and RELIABLE friend I know.

Going Deeper

Observation: What is the writer of Proverbs saying *{Look for key words, doctrines, unique phrases}?*

Interpretation: What does it mean? *{If you are doing a word study you may want to use a concordance. If you are studying a doctrine (a Biblical principle), can you give it a name? i.e., "the doctrine of . . . "}*

Application: What is God is saying to my heart? What is my next step in applying this truth? *{This is a key part of your Bible study. Read and pray through the Proverb again and review your thoughts on your notes on Observation and Interpretation then write out a concise personal application.}*

Proclamation: Take a moment. Ponder this and pray. Then answer this question: Who needs to hear this insight from me?

Personal Journal Notes And Prayer Concerns

DAY TWENTY-TWO: "The Predictable Life"

Today May You . . . treat everyone you meet with impeccable fairness.

False weights and unequal measures —
the Lord detests double standards of every kind. (Proverbs 20:10 NLT).

Turn your *Declaration Of Quality Wisdom* into this prayer of commitment:

Lord Jesus, *Today May I* treat everyone I meet with impeccable fairness.

 **Going Deeper**

Observation: What is the writer of Proverbs saying *{Look for key words, doctrines, unique phrases}?*

Interpretation: What does it mean? *{If you are doing a word study you may want to use a concordance. If you are studying a doctrine (a Biblical principle), can you give it a name? i.e., "the doctrine of . . . "}*

Application: What is God is saying to my heart? What is my next step in applying this truth? *{This is a key part of your Bible study. Read and pray through the Proverb again and review your thoughts on your notes on Observation and Interpretation then write out a concise personal application.}*

Proclamation: Take a moment. Ponder this and pray. Then answer this question: Who needs to hear this insight from me?

Personal Journal Notes And Prayer Concerns

DAY TWENTY-THREE: "Treasure Trove"

Today May You . . . make it your treasure to embrace words that add value to you and to everyone who hears you speak.

Wise words are more valuable
than much gold and many rubies. (Proverbs 20:15 NLT).

Turn your *Declaration Of Quality Wisdom* into this prayer of commitment:

Lord Jesus, *Today May I* make it my treasure to embrace words that add value to me and to everyone who hears me speak.

 **Going Deeper**

Observation: What is the writer of Proverbs saying *{Look for key words, doctrines, unique phrases}?*

Interpretation: What does it mean? *{If you are doing a word study you may want to use a concordance. If you are studying a doctrine (a Biblical principle), can you give it a name? i.e., "the doctrine of . . . "}*

Application: What is God is saying to my heart? What is my next step in applying this truth? *{This is a key part of your Bible study. Read and pray through the Proverb again and review your thoughts on your notes on Observation and Interpretation then write out a concise personal application.}*

Proclamation: Take a moment. Ponder this and pray. Then answer this question: Who needs to hear this insight from me?

Personal Journal Notes And Prayer Concerns

DAY TWENTY-FOUR: "Strategic Plans To Win"

Today May You . . . be selective and only fight the battles you can win.

Plans succeed through good counsel;

don't go to war without wise advice. (Proverbs 20:18 NLT).

Turn your *Declaration Of Quality Wisdom* into this prayer of commitment:

Lord Jesus, *Today May I* be selective and only fight the battles I can win.

 **Going Deeper**

Observation: What is the writer of Proverbs saying *{Look for key words, doctrines, unique phrases}?*

Interpretation: What does it mean? *{If you are doing a word study you may want to use a concordance. If you are studying a doctrine (a Biblical principle), can you give it a name? i.e., "the doctrine of . . . "}*

Application: What is God is saying to my heart? What is my next step in applying this truth? *{This is a key part of your Bible study. Read and pray through the Proverb again and review your thoughts on your notes on Observation and Interpretation then write out a concise personal application.}*

Proclamation: Take a moment. Ponder this and pray. Then answer this question: Who needs to hear this insight from me?

Personal Journal Notes And Prayer Concerns

DAY TWENTY-FIVE: "Guarding Yourself From The Garbage"

Today May You . . . GUARD what your EARS hear so that toxic WORDS will not leave your MOUTH.

A gossip goes around telling secrets,

so don't hang around with chatterers. (Proverbs 20:19 NLT).

Turn your *Declaration Of Quality Wisdom* into this prayer of commitment:

Lord Jesus, ***Today May I*** GUARD what my EARS hear so that toxic WORDS will not leave my MOUTH.

 **Going Deeper**

Observation: What is the writer of Proverbs saying *{Look for key words, doctrines, unique phrases}?*

Interpretation: What does it mean? *{If you are doing a word study you may want to use a concordance. If you are studying a doctrine (a Biblical principle), can you give it a name? i.e., "the doctrine of . . . "}*

Application: What is God is saying to my heart? What is my next step in applying this truth? *{This is a key part of your Bible study. Read and pray through the Proverb again and review your thoughts on your notes on Observation and Interpretation then write out a concise personal application.}*

Proclamation: Take a moment. Ponder this and pray. Then answer this question: Who needs to hear this insight from me?

Personal Journal Notes And Prayer Concerns

DAY TWENTY-SIX: "The Right Company You Keep Will Keep You Safe"

Today May You . . . GUARD your heart so you will not LOSE your soul.

Don't befriend angry people
or associate with hot-tempered people,
or you will learn to be like them
and endanger your soul. (Proverbs 22:24-25 NLT).

Turn your *Declaration Of Quality Wisdom* into this prayer of commitment:

Lord Jesus, ***Today May I*** GUARD my heart so I will not LOSE my soul.

 **Going Deeper**

Observation: What is the writer of Proverbs saying *{Look for key words, doctrines, unique phrases}?*

Interpretation: What does it mean? *{If you are doing a word study you may want to use a concordance. If you are studying a doctrine (a Biblical principle), can you give it a name? i.e., "the doctrine of . . . "}*

Application: What is God is saying to my heart? What is my next step in applying this truth? *{This is a key part of your Bible study. Read and pray through the Proverb again and review your thoughts on your notes on Observation and Interpretation then write out a concise personal application.}*

Proclamation: Take a moment. Ponder this and pray. Then answer this question: Who needs to hear this insight from me?

Personal Journal Notes And Prayer Concerns

DAY TWENTY-SEVEN: "The Fine Art Of Accepting Constructive Criticism"

Today May You . . . be WILLING to hear a CONSTRUCTIVE CRITIQUE from those who are WILLING to tell you the TRUTH about yourself.

An open rebuke is better than hidden love! Wounds from a sincere friend are better than many kisses from an enemy. (Proverbs 27:5-6 NLT).

Turn your *Declaration Of Quality Wisdom* into this prayer of commitment:

Lord Jesus, ***Today May I*** be WILLING to hear a CONSTRUCTIVE CRITIQUE from those who are WILLING to tell me the TRUTH about myself.

 **Going Deeper**

Observation: What is the writer of Proverbs saying *{Look for key words, doctrines, unique phrases}?*

Interpretation: What does it mean? *{If you are doing a word study you may want to use a concordance. If you are studying a doctrine (a Biblical principle), can you give it a name? i.e., "the doctrine of . . ."}*

Application: What is God is saying to my heart? What is my next step in applying this truth? *{This is a key part of your Bible study. Read and pray through the Proverb again and review your thoughts on your notes on Observation and Interpretation then write out a concise personal application.}*

Proclamation: Take a moment. Ponder this and pray. Then answer this question: Who needs to hear this insight from me?

Personal Journal Notes And Prayer Concerns

DAY TWENTY-EIGHT: "Loving The Sweet Life"

Today May You . . . LISTEN and LEARN from those who LOVE you so that you may live a SWEET LIFE.

The heartfelt counsel of a friend
is as sweet as perfume and incense. (Proverbs 27:9 NLT).

Turn your *Declaration Of Quality Wisdom* into this prayer of commitment:

Lord Jesus, ***Today May I*** LISTEN and LEARN from those who LOVE me so that I may live a SWEET LIFE.

 **Going Deeper**

Observation: What is the writer of Proverbs saying *{Look for key words, doctrines, unique phrases}?*

Interpretation: What does it mean? *{If you are doing a word study you may want to use a concordance. If you are studying a doctrine (a Biblical principle), can you give it a name? i.e., "the doctrine of . . . "}*

Application: What is God is saying to my heart? What is my next step in applying this truth? *{This is a key part of your Bible study. Read and pray through the Proverb again and review your thoughts on your notes on Observation and Interpretation then write out a concise personal application.}*

Proclamation: Take a moment. Ponder this and pray. Then answer this question: Who needs to hear this insight from me?

Personal Journal Notes And Prayer Concerns

DAY TWENTY-NINE: "Fanclub"

Today May You . . . cultivate the kinds of friendships that when everything hits the fan your friends will be your biggest fans.

Never abandon a friend—either yours or your father's. When disaster strikes, you won't have to ask your brother for assistance. It's better to go to a neighbor than to a brother who lives far away. (Proverbs 27:10 NLT).

Turn your *Declaration Of Quality Wisdom* into this prayer of commitment:

Lord Jesus, *Today May I* be on the lookout for sharp friends who will make me sharper and don't allow dull acquaintances to suck the life out of me and make me lose my edge.

 **Going Deeper**

Observation: What is the writer of Proverbs saying *{Look for key words, doctrines, unique phrases}?*

Interpretation: What does it mean? *{If you are doing a word study you may want to use a concordance. If you are studying a doctrine (a Biblical principle), can you give it a name? i.e., "the doctrine of . . . "}*

Application: What is God is saying to my heart? What is my next step in applying this truth? *{This is a key part of your Bible study. Read and pray through the Proverb again and review your thoughts on your notes on Observation and Interpretation then write out a concise personal application.}*

Proclamation: Take a moment. Ponder this and pray. Then answer this question: Who needs to hear this insight from me?

Personal Journal Notes And Prayer Concerns

DAY THIRTY: "The Sharp Life"

Today May You . . . be on the lookout for sharp friends who will make you sharper and don't allow dull acquaintances to suck the life out of you and make you lose your edge.

As iron sharpens iron,

so a friend sharpens a friend. (Proverbs 27:17 NLT).

Turn your *Declaration Of Quality Wisdom* into this prayer of commitment:

Lord Jesus, ***Today May I*** be on the lookout for sharp friends who will make me sharper and don't allow dull acquaintances to suck the life out of me and make me lose my edge.

 **Going Deeper**

Observation: What is the writer of Proverbs saying *{Look for key words, doctrines, unique phrases}?*

Interpretation: What does it mean? *{If you are doing a word study you may want to use a concordance. If you are studying a doctrine (a Biblical principle), can you give it a name? i.e., "the doctrine of . . . "}*

Application: What is God is saying to my heart? What is my next step in applying this truth? *{This is a key part of your Bible study. Read and pray through the Proverb again and review your thoughts on your notes on Observation and Interpretation then write out a concise personal application.}*

Proclamation: Take a moment. Ponder this and pray. Then answer this question: Who needs to hear this insight from me?

Personal Journal Notes And Prayer Concerns

DAY THIRTY-ONE: "Why Encouragement Is Superior To Flattery"

Today May You . . . be INTENTIONAL in your ENCOURAGEMENT towards your friends and build them up; resist the urge to FLATTER them and fatten up their pride and ego.

To flatter friends
is to lay a trap for their feet. (Proverbs 29:5 NLT).

Turn your *Declaration Of Quality Wisdom* into this prayer of commitment:

Lord Jesus, ***Today May I*** be INTENTIONAL in my ENCOURAGEMENT towards my friends and build them up; and resist the urge to FLATTER them and fatten up their pride and ego.

 **Going Deeper**

Observation: What is the writer of Proverbs saying *{Look for key words, doctrines, unique phrases}?*

Interpretation: What does it mean? *{If you are doing a word study you may want to use a concordance. If you are studying a doctrine (a Biblical principle), can you give it a name? i.e., "the doctrine of . . . "}*

Application: What is God is saying to my heart? What is my next step in applying this truth? *{This is a key part of your Bible study. Read and pray through the Proverb again and review your thoughts on your notes on Observation and Interpretation then write out a concise personal application.}*

Proclamation: Take a moment. Ponder this and pray. Then answer this question: Who needs to hear this insight from me?

Personal Journal Notes And Prayer Concerns

Summary: 31 Prayers Of Commitment / Action Points

Exercise: Set aside a block of time where you can pray, uninterrupted, these 31 prayers. Don't just "read" through them. Instead, pray, ponder, and reflect upon each one. To make it even more profound, pray these prayers outloud. Allow the intimate presence of the Lord flow over your heart as you pray.

Lord Jesus, *Today May I* make it my goal to ADD VALUE to everyone I meet.

Lord Jesus, *Today May I* be willing to SPEAK the truth and ENCOURAGE my friends to make the kinds of choices that will add great VALUE to them.

Lord Jesus, *Today May I* THINK good thoughts, do good DEEDS, and make a good CONTRIBUTION to my community.

Lord Jesus, *Today May I* add value to others by how I PLAN and by what I SAY.

Lord Jesus, *Today May I* be INTENTIONAL on using wise words and working hard so I may be SUCCESSFUL.

Lord Jesus, *Today May I* have a HEART of HUMILITY that will be open to ADVICE So that I can SUCCEED.

Lord Jesus, *Today May I* be WISE enough to listen to the advice of WISE people and make WISE decisions that will be a blessing to me.

Lord Jesus, *Today May I* before I do anything, THINK, PRAY, LISTEN, and then ACT.

Lord Jesus, *Today May I* have an open MIND to learn more, an open HEART to change more and an open LIFE to show more of God's grace at work in me.

Lord Jesus, *Today May I* always get better advice than my own.

Lord Jesus, *Today May I* say the RIGHT THING at the RIGHT TIME in the RIGHT WAY to the RIGHT PERSON.

Lord Jesus, *Today May I* make sure every word I use builds someone up and does not take them down.

Lord Jesus, *Today May I* FORGIVE when I find a FAULT, LOVE when I would rather LASH out, and GIVE GRACE because I need it too.

Lord Jesus, *Today May I* be willing to receive CORRECTION when a CORRECTION is needed.

Lord Jesus, *Today May I* control my tongue so my life may be flooded with peace.

Lord Jesus, *Today May I* be the kind of friend I need to be for me.

Lord Jesus, *Today May I* not allow my HEART to get ahead of my HEAD or I might lose more than my MIND.

Lord Jesus, *Today May I* protect the relationships that are important to me by winning their love, not by winning the argument.

Lord Jesus, *Today May I* be the kind of trusted friend my intimate circle of friends needs from me.

Lord Jesus, *Today May I* be a GOOD FRIEND by being a GOOD LISTENER so I will be able to give GOOD ADVICE that will help my friend have a GOOD DAY.

Lord Jesus, *Today May I* be the most LOYAL and RELIABLE friend I know.

Lord Jesus, *Today May I* treat everyone I meet with impeccable fairness.

Lord Jesus, *Today May I* make it my treasure to embrace words that add value to me and to everyone who hears me speak.

Lord Jesus, *Today May I* be selective and only fight the battles I can win.

Lord Jesus, *Today May I* GUARD what my EARS hear so that toxic WORDS will not leave my MOUTH.

Lord Jesus, *Today May I* GUARD my heart so I will not LOSE my soul.

Lord Jesus, *Today May I* be WILLING to hear a CONSTRUCTIVE CRITIQUE from those who are WILLING to tell me the TRUTH about myself.

Lord Jesus, *Today May I* LISTEN and LEARN from those who LOVE me so that I may live a SWEET LIFE.

Lord Jesus, *Today May I* be on the lookout for sharp friends who will make me sharper and don't allow dull acquaintances to suck the life out of me and make me lose my edge.

Lord Jesus, *Today May I* be on the lookout for sharp friends who will make me sharper and don't allow dull acquaintances to suck the life out of me and make me lose my edge.

Lord Jesus, *Today May I* be INTENTIONAL in my ENCOURAGEMENT towards my friends and build them up; and resist the urge to FLATTER them and fatten up their pride and ego.

HOW YOU CAN HAVE
A RELATIONSHIP WITH JESUS

✓ GOD LOVES YOU AND HAS A WONDERFUL PLAN FOR YOUR LIFE

For I know the plans I have for you," declares the LORD, "plans to prosper you and not to harm you, plans to give you hope and a future. **Jeremiah 29:11 (NIV)**

✓ AS A RESULT OF MAN GOING HIS OWN WAY AND REJECTING GOD, A CHASM, A GREAT DIVIDE, HAS COME SEPARATING A JUST AND HOLY GOD FROM SINFUL MAN

for all have sinned and fall short of the glory of God, **Romans 3:23 (NIV)**

For the wages of sin is death, but the gift of God is eternal life in Christ Jesus our Lord. **Romans 6:23 (NIV)**

✓ GOD SENT HIS SON, HIS PERFECT SON TO BECOME OUR SACRIFICE. HE WHO IS SINLESS TOOK UPON HIMSELF OUR SINS, OFFERING TO RESTORE OUR BROKEN RELATIONSHIP WITH GOD, BRIDGING THE GAP BETWEEN GOD AND MAN

We all, like sheep, have gone astray, each of us has turned to his own way; and the LORD has laid on him the iniquity of us all. **Isaiah 53:6 (NIV)**

The next day John saw Jesus coming toward him and said, "Look, the Lamb of God, who takes away the sin of the world!" **John 1:29 (NIV)**

✓ GOD HAS GIVEN EACH MAN A CHOICE EITHER TO ACCEPT THE FREE GIFT OF SALVATION AND LIVE FOREVER OR TO REJECT HIS GRACIOUS GIFT AND SPEND ETERNITY FOREVER SEPARATED FROM GOD

For God so loved the world that he gave his one and only Son, that whoever believes in him shall not perish but have eternal life. **John 3:16 (NIV)**

[12]Yet to all who received him, to those who believed in his name, he gave the right to become children of God-- [13]children born not of natural descent, nor of human decision or a husband's will, but born of God. **John 1:12-13 (NIV)**

Essential Spiritual Growth Resources from
Something New Christian Publishers
and Quality Leadership Consultants

Websites, Newsletter, and Blogs:

www.dennybates.com and www.ReallyGoodDay4U.com is the hub for all of our teaching and coaching resources. Check out our free downloads as well as our store.

www.thequalitydisciple.com links to dennybates.com.

www.qualityleadershipconsultants.com links to dennybates.com.

www.thequalitydisciple.blogspot.com is the teaching blog for Psalms of Discipleship.

www.facebook.com/denny.bates is my portal to social networking.

Dr. Denny Bates and Quality Leadership Tips For You is my newsletter. Featured leadership articles, devotional thoughts, and a menu of coaching and book resources.

Sign up at http://www.dennybates.com You can follow me on Twitter @dennybates

Books:

Other titles from the Quality Discipleship Series:
- ❖ How To Study And Apply The Bible To Your Life (PDF Book only)
- ❖ Growing Up…Practical Bible Studies For New And Growing Christians (PDF Book only)
- ❖ Psalms of Discipleship: A One Year Journey With The Shepherd (Kindle or printed copy)
- ❖ Christmas Meditations of Worship: Four Weeks of Advent (Kindle or printed copy)
- ❖ Living Above The Fray: Learning The Seven Healthy Leadership Principles That Will Shelter You From The Destructive Effects Of Leader-I-Tis (Kindle or printed copy)
- ❖ My Spiritual Life Plan: Creating An Effective Spiritual Life Plan For The Quality Disciple (Kindle or printed copy)
- ❖ Living Above The Fray Leadership Assessment: The Coaches Guide For Leading With Quality In Mind (Kindle or printed copy)
- ❖ Building A Christian Community Of Friends: Four Practical Studies On Biblical Friendships (Kindle or printed copy)
- ❖ Changing Places: Understanding The Process Of Transition. (Kindle or printed copy)
- ❖ Life-Ol-Ogy: Mastering The Study Of Your Life, Your Team, Your Profession and Your Customers (Kindle or printed copy)
- ❖ Growing In Greatness: *31 Living Legacy Principles From the Proverbs For the Quality Leader (Proverbs 1:1-5:14), Volume 1* (Kindle or printed copy)

- ❖ Quality Wisdom For A Modern Age: The Wisdom Book Of Proverbs (Kindle or printed copy)
- ❖ How To Have A Really Good Day With The GOS-PILL During Times Of Crisis: 31 Days Of Inspiration (Kindle or printed copy)
- ❖ Coming in 2020!!! Living Beyond The Fray: *How Bitter Busters Can Set You Free From Becoming Bitter Against Family, Friends, Career, Church and God.*"

Retreat Journals:
- ❖ The Power – Broker's Guide To The Kingdom
- ❖ Four Legacies For A Life Change
- ❖ Three Commitments That Change A Life
- ❖ Growing In Grace: A Fresh Look At Biblical Discipleship
- ❖ Adding Quality To Your Life

Help Me Write My Story Books (A ghost writing and book coaching custom service)

For information see next page or connect to www.HelpMeWriteMyStory.com.

- ❖ "Touched by Him: A Man Who Said Yes To Jesus" by Harry F. Lyles as told
  to Dr. Denny Bates (Unpublished)
- ❖ "I'm Just Rebeckah Wilhelmina And I Found A Way Out" by Rebeckah Wilhelmina (Healthy Curves Count Publishers)
- ❖ "The Blue Duck: Learning How To Discover Your Competitive Edge And Celebrate The Uniqueness Of You" by Sandra Mason (Younique Publishers)
- ❖ "How To Kick Your Own Butt: The Fine Art Of Leading Yourself Well" by Carol Mabe (CMC Transformational Publishing)
- ❖ "My Life: Then And Now: Won't He Do It" by Karen Calhoun (KMJC Publishers)
- ❖ "More Than A Seed: The Yearn For God's Children To Accept, Grow, And Fight" by Akayla Frazier (Changed Legacy Publishing)
- ❖ "Take the Soap" by Bryan Braddock, Byon "kNOw Ca$h" McCullough as told to Dr. Denny Bates (Take The Soap Publishers—Coming soon)

Contact us for availability and cost.
www.dennybates.com

What is your story?

Help Me Write My Story (HMWMS)
www.HelpMeWriteMyStory.com

HELP ME WRITE MY STORY is a highly relational, process-driven, professional service that empowers an aspiring author to produce a personal memoir that is shared in a self-published book (including Kindle too). HELP ME WRITE MY STORY helps you to focus on this acrostic:

H = **Heartfelt** (The best place to begin writing your story is in the HEART)

M = **Memories** (If you do not WRITE THEM DOWN you will eventually FORGET many of them)

W = **Well-spoken** (To tell your story you've got to be a CLEAR COMMUNICATOR so you will be understood)

M = **Motivational** (It's important for you not to only share with your readers how CHALLENGING your circumstances may have been but it's even more important to share how you faced your obstacles and got through them SUCCESSFULLY)

S = **Strategic** (Your story will most likely not speak to everyone, but it will speak to SOMEONE, so it's important to know WHO you are seeking to influence the most and why)

I believe that our lives are the sum of many stories filled with adventures, wonders, disappointments, successes, tragedies, victories, and mysteries. Our **STORIES**, all of them, have the necessary components for a lasting legacy.

Your story is a **GIFT** to others. Your life is a **STEWARDSHIP**. Your story matters because **YOU MATTER**. Your story needs to be **SHARED** with and **REMEMBERED** by those who need to KNOW your story.

That said, many **STORIES** never go beyond the back of our minds and fade away forever. And that is why I am writing to you. I want to help you **WRITE YOUR STORY**.

IMAGINE for a moment what you could do with **YOUR STORY** in the **FORM** of a **BOOK**:

- **YOUR STORY**, in the form of a quality published book, becomes something tangible and is in your hands.

- **YOUR STORY** can give encouragement to others, especially to your family, friends, and customers/clients, and even to people you will unlikely ever meet in this life.

- **YOUR STORY** contains your legacy and will always be there, even after you are long gone, influencing future readers.

- **YOUR STORY**, in the form of a book, will be the perfect and unique item for you to give away or sell, creating a new revenue stream.

- **YOUR STORY** can serve as a mentor to help the person who wants to learn how to apply the life lessons you experienced.

YOUR STORY matters to you and **YOUR STORY** matters to me too.

What is HELP ME WRITE MY STORY?

HELP ME WRITE MY STORY coaches the author client through each creative phase of writing a book:

- How to create the Big Story Idea
- How to create a *Write My Story Time Line*
- How to do great research
- How to create a strong outline of chapters and subchapters
- How to use creative words to paint vivid mental and emotional images
- How to tell your story in an interesting way
- How to write strong chapter summaries
- How to create of book title and subtitle that resonates with the reader
- How to create a book front and back cover that catches the reader's attention
- How to write back cover copy
- How to take an author's story to the finished product in print and in Kindle formats.
- How to use the power of social networking to promote your story

Who needs HELP ME WRITE MY STORY?

HELP ME WRITE MY STORY can be a great resource for the person who . . .

- Wants to write their story but need practical instruction, intentional coaching and accountability.
- Wants to make sure their story, their legacy, is preserved in a format so family members and friends will remember and be inspired by their story.

- Wants to use their story as a way to open doors of future opportunities for even greater influence.

- Wants a personal product to either sell or gift to others.

- Wants the rewarding satisfaction of having a professional copy of their personal story.

How does HELP ME WRITE MY STORY work?

Each writing project has its own unique set of challenges, but I've sought to present three different packages and pricing levels. All five are dependent upon the pace, progress, and extraordinary challenges of the book.

There are five Story Coaching service levels of Help Me Write My Story*:

In addition to the fees for each package, a reduced monthly payment plus a percentage of the royalties is an alternative form of payment. See me for the details.

Help Me Write My Story Books is a ghost writing and book coaching custom service. For information connect to www.HelpMeWriteMyStory.com

QUALITY LEADERSHIP CONSULTANTS

PROFESSIONAL COACHING, CONSULTING,
AND TEACHING
*Presenting **Quality** Ideas;*
*Producing **Quality** Leaders*

Introducing Dr. Denny Bates
Professional Life, Business Coach, Teacher, Writer, Speaker And Consultant

Why is it important for you to have a professional quality life coach and leadership trainer?

It has been said, "Experience is the best guide in life." The truth is *guided experience* is the best guide! Time, money, and emotional energy can be saved by linking up with a person who already understands where you are, where you want to go and has a good grasp on how to lead you there in a positive way.

What kind of guided experience do I offer?

Seasoned in both the market place and non-profit settings, I can offer you and/or your organization Quality Leadership coaching tracks with a relational emphasis. For instance: Personal Growth, Communication Skills, Building Healthy Relationships, Career Counseling / Job Performance, Life Transitions, Organizational Health; and for faith-based individuals and/or organizations, Spiritual Growth. My practical experience in both for-profit and non-profit settings, coupled with my academic and professional training, affords me the ability to offer you unique Quality Leadership services.

The JOHN MAXWELL **Team**

AN INDEPENDENT CERTIFIED COACH, TEACHER AND SPEAKER
WITH THE JOHN MAXWELL TEAM

My friend John Maxwell says,

"Everything rises and falls on leadership"

As a Leadership Specialist, I can help YOU in the marketplace!

✓ With years of experience working as a manager in the marketplace, I know what it takes to create a healthy organization. I can train your leaders and employees in effective teamwork and communication.

✓ I know how to help business leaders practice the kind of self-care that not only benefits them personally, but also adds value to the company.

✓ I know how to help a management team build a culture that places great value on integrity and success.

✓ I can help you and your leaders set reasonable goals and show you the tools to help you reach each one.

✓ I can help you reproduce your values, vision and passion in the lives of others.

✓ I can help you sharpen your leadership skills in a group coaching setting or one to one. As a professional life coach and leadership trainer, I can offer you the finest coaching and training resources available today as a certified coach, teacher and speaker for the John Maxwell Team.

Email dennybates@gmail.com
www.dennybates.com

What does a Disciple-Making Ministry look like?
It looks like . . .

SOMETHING *new*

"Do not call to mind the former things, or ponder things of the past; Behold, I will do something new . . ."
Isaiah 43:18, 19a

- Is a ministry that focuses upon making Quality disciples for Jesus

- Is a ministry that encourages believers to connect in community and experience the discipled life

- Is a ministry that seeks to help other body of believers to learn how to live the discipled life through seminars, workshops, keynote speaking and interactive coaching

Contact Dr. Denny Bates for more information on how you and your church can create a culture of DiscipleMakers4Jesus

www.TheQualityDisciple.com

What Others Are Saying About My Leadership Coaching And Discipleship Via DiscipleMakers4Jesus (DM4J)

I know and have worked with Denny Bates for more than a decade. Denny now serves as a leadership trainer and coach. It is my pleasure to recommend Denny as a valuable and trusted resource for leadership training and coaching. In addition to earning his doctoral degree in leadership, Denny is also an independent certified coach, teacher, and speaker for The John Maxwell Team. I believe you and your organization will benefit from his knowledge of what leaders need in order to grow as a leader. You will appreciate Denny's relational approach to leadership training and his ability to connect with people. Dr. Bates offers workshops, seminars, keynote speaking, and coaching ... aiding your personal and professional growth through study and practical application of John Maxwell's leadership methods. **(President and CEO of Regional Hospital)**

Just wanted to let you know how much our time of coaching and leadership development has meant to me. Every time I am faced with a challenge I try to walk thru the Grace tree of wisdom. You set the example every day of the man of God I want to be. Thank you! **(Corporate Manager of Medical Services)**

[I've learned] to keep the main thing the main thing!! To take care of the people that God puts in front of me everyday. **(Sales Manager of automotive dealership)**

Denny has been my friend, pastor, colleague, mentor and confidant for almost 10 years. During this time, Denny has led me through tough waters, given me wise counsel and taught me practical ways to live out my faith while falling more in love with my Savior. **(Youth Pastor)**

Other than my own father, Denny has been my most trusted friend and spiritual mentor. Denny's discipleship has been truly transforming and helped me to realize the importance of investing in others as he has invested in me. **(Medical Device Consultant)**

I treasure my relationship with Denny because we share a common heart to help people discover all that Christ wants to do in and through them. **(Disciple-Making Missionary to Eastern Europe)**

I have known Denny for many years and have had the privilege to work with him on the same pastoral staff for over 5 years. During that time I have sought Denny's counsel on many issues ranging from personal struggles to theological questions. Denny has always provided me with poignant, gracious and thoughtful counsel. They say that everyone should have a mentor and I am blessed to be able to consider Denny my mentor. He has been an invaluable asset in my life and ministry. **(Clinical Counselor)**

My relationship with Denny has been personal, honest, and Christ-centered. Denny's common sense approach to the issues of life is always soundly based on scriptural principles. I remember discussing with Denny how I felt that I needed to do so much service for the Lord because of all the times I had failed Him. Denny gently said to me, "It's all about grace". I was reminded that there is no 'payback' plan for the Lord. **(Pastor)**

Having a group of peers who candidly discuss the awesome responsibility that each carries as a servant and hearing how God has responded so richly to our needs clearly demonstrates how marvelous is our God, who works in each of our lives to do His will. **(Hospital Vice-President in a discipleship group for executives)**

Denny and I have know each other for nearly fifteen years, we bonded shortly after he had his heart attack because of an illness I had years prior – Guillain-Barre Syndrome – that made me more aware of the right priorities I should have in life. Through this episode and having children similar in age we bonded in a unique and special way rarely achieved between men. Approximately one year ago I lost my job as a senior executive at a large international company that I had been with 26 years, during the transition period of me finding another job Denny was an extreme encouragement to me. During a time when I was wrestling between accepting a position or not and I will never forget what Denny told me "You can just accept it as God's providential care". He was right! I later humbly accepted the position as President & Chief Operating Officer for a Subsea Oilfield Manufacturing company. **(Corporate Executive)**

Denny has been a teacher / mentor / discipler / encourager / prayer partner and great friend who God has used to help me keep a godly perspective on the different times & issues of life I've gone through as I've seek to follow Jesus. Once while praying with Denny through a career move, he encouraged me to think of the gifts & skills I had and then ask what I had a passion for, and then to ask God to show me how they can fit together. From this I learned to stop putting these gifts & skills in a "Box" and limiting what God could do with them, and use them for. For the first time, as I now work for a non-profit Christian organization as a warehouse manager, I feel I'm using the gifts and abilities God has given me to fulfill His purpose at something I really have a passion for! **(Former market place worker, now Missionary who is impacting the world)**

Denny met with me at 7 a.m. every Friday for a year. He came to me knowing he would receive my weekly burdens. This is not the way any of us would choose to begin our day. He does not judge nor do I ever feel judged. He is one of the most selfless and giving person I have ever met. This is easy to say because I know he is just a man. His obedience to God sets him apart. He taught me to live by grace, be long suffering, and love my wife regardless of my excuses. **(Medical Worker, Physical therapist assistant)**

Through a lifestyle of disciple making, Denny Bates has shown me what it truly means to live out Matthew 28: 19, 20. **(Educator)**

I've heard it said that on this side of eternity that there are only two things that you can be certain of: death and taxes. I'm certain of three things; the first two and that I have a friend in Denny Bates! I asked God at the beginning of my ministry to bring solid men into my life that would disciple me, teach me and hold me accountable. Denny has been an extreme answer to that prayer. **(Church-planting Pastor)**

Dr. Denny Bates opened my eyes to the power of small groups. He showed me what a true mentor really is. I will be forever grateful for his leadership, friendship, and love! **(Videographer)**

Practical application of God's teachings by normal, everyday family men such as myself; that's what DM4J means to me. Listening to and sharing the innumerable ways the Lord touches the lives of each and every man in this group is not only uplifting, but inspiring. From the greatest trials to what might seem trivial, God has a plan and a purpose for it all. The value of DM4J to me is immeasurable. **(Pharmacist)**

Praise For Quality Wisdom For A Modern Age:

For me, reading from the book of Proverbs has always felt a bit like trying to drink water from a fire hydrant - too much comes at me at one time and it overwhelms me. In *Quality Living For a Modern Age*, Dr. Denny Bates has meticulously broken down this powerful, timeless Old Testament book of wise instruction into day by day "bite size" truths enabling the reader to apply each truth and get the very most out of the Scriptures. The *Prayer of Commitment* found at the end of each devotion is guaranteed to help the reader in their personal growth. This is one book you will not want to hurry through. It's great for family devotions as well.
~ Kirby King, inspirational speaker and Bible teacher; author of *Abiding in Christ: What Is it Anyway?* and *Walking Through Fire Without Getting Burned: Finding Hope In The Hard Places*

Dr. Denny Bates has a fabulous unique way to share his wealth of quality wisdom with his readers. The devotions will lift, stretch, encourage, and press you forward. Your strongest challenge may very well be the fact that you don't want to part ways and lay the book down. Just as there is a Proverbs chapter for every day of the month, this devotional will provide you with what I like to call the icing on the cake. As you begin your journey you will want to keep this book close by at all times!
~ Carol Mabe, Life Coach, Leadership Trainer, Speaker, Author of *Kick Your Own Butt: The Fine Art Of Leading Yourself Well*

Denny Bates's *Quality Wisdom for A Modern Age* is valuable for two reasons. One, it lays our Christian principles that professionals can immediately apply to their career. Two, it is an ongoing resource of daily encouragement that can be used by new and seasoned Christians alike.
~ Traci McCombs, Author and Blogger

What a wonderful daily encouragement! Dr. Denny Bates has dissected the book of Proverbs to highlight the wisdom God has provided for us in this great book of the Bible. I believe this daily devotional will help you apply Proverbs' eternal truths in a more practical and relevant way that will assist you in your everyday Christian walk. I highly recommend *Quality Wisdom for a Modern Age* for your daily study of God's Word.
~ Ron Lyles
Owner, Schofield's Hardware and Sporting Goods
Board Trustee, Leadership Ministries Worldwide

The book of Proverbs is a phenomenal book. It is such an inspiration on what, where, who God is. It helps in our daily walk. It gives you strength, wisdom, discernment for life. It gives practical ways to look at life through God's lenses. I would highly recommend *Quality Wisdom for a Modern Age.*
~ Cleo Corey, author and life coach

Denny inspires me. His thoughts captured in this book will warm your heart and challenge your mind. Get ready to consume fresh words of wisdom.
~ Kary Oberbrunner, author of *Your Secret Name, the Deeper Path, and Day Job to Dream Job*

I love the book of Proverbs. I love how you quote and simplify the meaning of each verse to give an easy understanding of this great book. Any person who reads your book will be helped by being able to apply scripture to reality. Absolutely incredible book Denny. God bless you.
~ Traceyann Pearl Brough, author of *Heaven's Got A Plan For You*

You will find that as you read this book your thoughts are transformed, and your emotions are empowered with life. God will meet you in it as you take the journey from one page into the next. I highly recommend because it is engaging, and you will gain insight to your daily life in an enjoyable way. He has presented challenges that are relatable with answers that are attainable.
~ Laura Harris, Artist, Design Director at No Other Wall

Proverbs is my favorite book in the Bible. Primarily because of its consistent message regarding wisdom. As a Christian business leader, I am responsible for leading my team and truly making a positive difference. I never want to come up short. God enables us with unique gifts/talents, but he holds us responsible to develop those talents; this book is a great place to start. I've known Denny for some time, and he has always been passionate about Christian leadership and helping those leaders do their very best in garnering the necessary wisdom to lead well.
~ Rick Saunders
President/CEO, First Reliance Bank

I remember the day I first met Denny Bates. It was his welcoming smile that made me think of Jesus. His humor and warmth put me at ease. I knew this would be someone I would collaborate with, share advice with, and enjoy as a longtime friend. With this new published work of his, *Quality Wisdom For A Modern Age*, I can see how Denny truly fathers others in the faith. He is a disciple-maker and this new book, and its easy-to-read format will help shape the next generation of believers.
~ Robin L. Lewis,
Author of *The Guts and Glory Of Forgiveness: Living Healed*, speaker, and Christ-centered life coach

I am a very simple thinker...I really enjoyed the 31 days....simple and short...to the point....easy for me to follow.
~ Wick Jackson
Envoy International, Director

In the short time I've known Denny, I have come to find him as a very dedicated man of God, who chooses daily to walk the high road, while encouraging everyone he meets to join him. Denny doesn't just offer you a kind word and send you on your way, but rather, he demonstrates a genuine interest in and concern for others ability to maneuver through the stuff of life and come out better for it on the other side. In his book, *Quality Wisdom For A Modern Age*, Denny delves into the Proverbs, unpacking the rich material contained therein, and has provided a concise and useful tool for us to apply these old Scriptural truths in todays "Modern Age." Whether you are looking for a quick reference guide or to dig deeper, I believe you have just found what you are looking for. Thank you, Denny, for sharing your love of the LORD with us, and for your desire to see others grow in His amazing Grace!
~ Leslie Rutten
Homemaker; Occupational Therapist

For anyone who desires to be obedient to the command "But prove yourselves doers of the word, and not merely hearers who delude themselves" (James 1:22 NASB) as it applies to the Book of Proverbs, then Denny's book will prove to be a well laid out tool. There are many useful resources included. The Subject Index alone makes the book worth having. It is a tremendous guide for topical searching.
Well done my friend,
~ Ron Bennett
Elder, Bible Teacher, Church at Sandhurst

Dr. Denny Bates has put together a simple, daily look at the promises of God that are declared in direction, woven to our souls in prayer. Men and women are transformed when they allow the living word of God to live in them. Each page of *Quality Wisdom For A Modern Age* is a promise of God, declared for today, brought to life in prayer. So that "Today May You" grow in the knowledge of the Greatness of God!
~ Dick Brown
Business Owner

In *Quality Wisdom For A Modern Age*, Dr. Denny Bates' commitment to make quality disciples for Jesus shines through in this collection of rich resources. If you desire to deepen your walk with Jesus and are looking for an easy to follow, systematic approach which also offers the flexibility of diving deeper, then look no more. Whether you desire a personal study or to make progress with others (QWMA) takes you on a journey through the wisdom of Proverbs, encouraging a closer walk with Jesus.
~ Lisa Ray
Retired Educator

James, the half-brother of Jesus, wrote under the inspiration of the Holy Spirit to the dispersed who were living in a world hostile to the gospel message ... "But if any of you lacks wisdom, let him ask of God, who gives to all generously and without reproach, and it will be given to him" (James 1:5). Dr. H. Dennis Bates or Denny, my spiritual brother as well as my biological sibling, has written a resource just for those that would seek God's wisdom in a world that is still hostile to His message. *Quality Wisdom for a Modern Age* is an easy to use exploration of King Solomon's masterpiece on wisdom, Proverbs. It can be used as a devotional, a small group study or a guide for wisdom on different aspects of life as the need arises. I am truly looking forward to using it in my daily life in this complicated, complex world and am thankful that Solomon had it right when he wrote that there was nothing new under the sun; Only the names and the places change. The human experience is just that, the human experience and it never changes.
~ Tamara Bates-Rhodes, RN

You know it's going to be a good day when you encounter some quality wisdom first thing, walk with it and let it guide you throughout your day. And so, it is with the daily *Declarations of Quality Wisdom* from the Proverbs-based devotional book, *Quality Wisdom for a Modern Age,* by Denny Bates. This guidebook gives you one piece of wisdom each day for you to savor and incorporate into your daily practice. In turn providing a basis for personal growth which will spill over into your professional and spiritual life. It gives you the opportunity to apply that wisdom and live it loudly. Remember, what we say is heard in what we show. So, walk with the wisdom in this devotional and grow in greatness.
~ Dennis Arnst, PhD - Audiologist

Dr. Denny Bates has created an exegesis of Proverbs that is both rich and practical, with clear encouragement about how to live wisely in a modern community of Faith. The Lord's words are like goads; spurring us on, teaching, and admonishing. Aptly applied, God's Word is alive, critical and precious, changing the trajectory of our lives. Denny's book draws a thoughtful picture of how to best glean from the Proverbs, and how to strategically do what they say. Thank you Denny for allowing yourself to be a scholar, brother, and even more so a son. When you sent this for me to read, the Lord meant it as a balm and direction for my heart. This book is dynamic and concise, Spirit led, and a daily treasure of wisdom!
~ Dee Hoehn, M.A., L.P.C. Owner and Therapist Grace Counseling, LLC

Proverbs is well known as the book of wisdom. Having the opportunity of seeing Denny's heart and service for the Lord, I know his wisdom and insight will carry his readers on a deeper dive. Get ready for the journey.
~ Dexter Godfrey, Kingdom Power Couple

'In a society where the wisdom of the Bible is continually being pushed aside, it is refreshing to see a book published that makes The Proverbs applicable. Denny's heart to see this generation embrace the Truth and direction of the Proverbs is a light to follow through Quality Wisdom for a Modern Age"
~ Debra Lynn Hayes, author *RISE....What To Do When Hell Won't Back Off*

Most won't admit that they need it, but everyone needs guidance in today's modern age. Full of wisdom and a burning desire to always help others, Denny Bates does a great job of delivering this wisdom in a simple format.
~ John Chase, Financial Advisor

Dr. Bates uses the book of Proverbs to give simple yet profound words for each daily devotional with much attention to detail giving the reader points to ponder throughout his day. A good read.
~ Pam Clemons, retired RN

"Living in this world, we need all the wisdom we can get! The Proverbs are chock full of applicable tidbits and Dr. Bates does an amazing job at breaking it down into bite-size bits that we can digest on a daily basis. I thoroughly enjoy his approach and see it as something that anyone can implement daily--over and over!"
~ Renee Vidor, speaker, and community-creator, author of *Measuring Up: How to WIN in a World of Comparison*

In *Quality Wisdom for a Modern Age*, Dr. Denny Bates has, once again, provided a million-dollar tool for followers of Christ to develop discipleship habits and to live Kingdom lives. This resource could be used in a variety of ways and is full of "high-value wisdom" about life, about living for God, about dealing with people, and about living with situations. This work is a guaranteed GRAND SLAM for every disciple of Christ!!!
Dr. David Wike, Pastor Ebenezer Baptist Church

Quality Wisdom For A Modern Age embraces the teachings of Solomon as written in Proverbs. Timely lessons that respect our schedules yet provide an in-depth challenge encouraging us to assimilate and connect with coworkers, friends, and seekers we meet on life's road. Whether you use it as a study guide or a future reference book for all things Proverbs; check it out.
Tessy L. Baker, Ed.S School Psychologist

Quality Wisdom For A Modern Age is an insightful read that shows you how to recognize and apply the truth on a daily basis. Dr. Denny Bates provides an amazing resource that brings the wisdom and practical teaching from the book of Proverbs to life. Make it a part of your routine as you grow, lead, serve, and impact the world.
~ Jim Zugschwert, speaker, coach, and author of *Peak Perspective*

If there is a writer who can take the ancient words of the book of Proverbs and help us apply them to our present days, that writer is Dr. Denny Bates. Quality Wisdom for a Modern Age will challenge you and bless you in your professional and personal life as Dr. Bates guides you in hearing Proverbs with enlightened spirit-led ears. This book is a must-have!
~ Helen Rogers Dobbins BSN, RN Blogger for Sorrow into Dancing

Your very practical encouragement has always been a bright spot for me. Thank you for sharing this! I can't wait to see how God will continue to use you!
~ Abby Feistel, mom and blogger

Denny is a great friend and mentor of mine and has been for nearly two decades. In *Quality Wisdom for a Modern Age* you will find insight, perspective and truth that is deeply needed for life in this world. I cannot recommend this book more highly to you. It is a must use resource as you journey through life.
~ Reeves Cannon, M.A.,LPC, BCPCC, Executive Pastor, Church at Sandhurst

Quality Wisdom for a Modern Age is not book on leadership – it is a manual on how to incorporate proverbs into our daily lives to not only deal with the issues of daily life, but to anticipate them. Keep the book close to your nightstand, to use the analogy "Break glass in case of emergency", or to be inspired. Dr. Denny Bates uses daily declarations to assist individuals and leaders to help them in their daily duties. This is important as one must be able to lead themselves in order to lead others.
~ Len Clark, Ph.D. LTC Media

"Denny has a clear talent for packaging encouraging, Biblical content in a form that anyone can benefit from. *Quality Wisdom For A Modern Age* is another winner in his lineup of materials that can be used for a variety of settings and applications. I'm thankful for his contributions to the Body of Christ!"
~ Chris Honeycutt Lead Pastor, Forward /// Myrtle Beach

Dr Denny Bates is consistent in publishing *quality* resources that we can apply in our real lives. *Quality Wisdom for a Modern Age* is no different. Denny pours his mentorship onto paper again so we can turn to daily use in practical ways to become better, *quality* leaders.
~ Bo Myers: Husband, Father, Local ministry leader, Servant pastor, Deputy Coroner

About Dr. Denny Bates

Dr. Denny Bates is Principal Consultant for Quality Leadership Consultants, founder of Something New Christian Publishers, adjunct faculty mentor in the Columbia Biblical Seminary online Doctor of Ministerial Leadership program, and a founding member of the John Maxwell Team of certified coaches, speakers, and trainers. He has earned degrees from Francis Marion College [B.S.] and Columbia Biblical Seminary and School of Missions [MDiv, DMin]. With a doctoral degree in personal and organizational leadership, he is well equipped to serve as teacher, life coach, mentor, disciplemaker, motivational speaker and writer for his own leadership and personal growth titles as well as helping others write their stories*

Denny has written for an international publisher of Bible commentary, served as the Discipleship Pastor in the local church, as well as being a leader in the marketplace by creating the social networking brand #Aisle31. By God's grace, he seeks to live above the fray and "Press on!" Visit **www.dennybates.com**.

*See www.HelpMeWriteMyStory.com for this custom service.

Made in the USA
Columbia, SC
17 April 2022

59108321R00057